MW00939752

andreaszlorjen.com
EXPLORE THE BEAUTY OF EXISTENCE.

SANKALPA

How to Understand and Manifest
your Innermost Desires

ANDREAS ZIÖRJEN

ISBN: 9781094701776

The contents of this book are based on the audio course "Sankalpa" created by the author
for publication on Insight Timer in 2018.

The original version of this book was published in 2019 titled

"Das Sankalpa-Handbuch (German edition)" on KDP

Translated by Andreas Ziörjen

DEDICATION

For my partner and best friend, Malu. May plenitude, ease and inner freedom in all areas of life always be with you.

CONTENTS

1 INTRODUCTION **1**

2 HOW DO WISHES ARISE? **5**

3 GET WHAT WE WANT—AND WANT WHAT WE HAVE... **15**

4 WHAT IS FREE WILL, REALLY? **23**

5 VISUALIZING THE OUTCOME **34**

6 NEEDS AND STRATEGIES **46**

7 GRATITUDE AND LETTING GO **59**

8 CREATING A SANKALPA **67**

9 APPLYING THE SANKALPA **82**

10 THE SANKALPA IN EVERYDAY LIFE **90**

11 TURNING WISHES INTO PREFERENCES **97**

12 THE SANKALPA LIST **103**

ABOUT THE AUTHOR **138**

ACKNOWLEDGEMENTS

As is the case with all my books, it would be impossible to mention all the wonderful people who directly or indirectly contributed to their creation. I am very grateful to all of you!

Nevertheless, I would like to express special gratitude to:

Isabelle Pikoern of Insight Timer, where much of the content of this practice book has been published in the form of a meditation course.

My yoga nidra and meditation teacher, Anna E. Röcker, who introduced me to *sankalpa* for the first time years ago.

My first Ho'oponopono teachers, Ulrich Duprée and Andrea Bruchacova, who fundamentally changed my view of the world for the better

Goddess Pele, and all the wonderful people on the island of Hawai'i, where the idea for this book was born.

1 INTRODUCTION

A wish, a desire—what is that, exactly? In yoga, we try to train our focus ever more on the present moment, thus, reach a state of restfulness in the mind, which ideally lies beyond the desire- and judgment-driven activity of our "thinking machine."

Yet, even if we manage to reach this state, we can never escape desire for long because having desires and objectives is a fundamental prerequisite of our life in this world. Therefore, since we cannot be genuinely free of desire, it is well worthwhile to at least work with our desires in a conscious way. How often are we really aware of what we want, and why?

Years ago, when I first started to observe and work with my desires in any depth for the first time, I was in for a little shock: I had to realize that many of my superficial wishes and goals, the realization of which I pursued day after day, were not actually my own. They were—and still, are, in part—ideas shaped by my environment, my family history and society as a whole about what is right and desirable—and, even more limiting, about what is even *possible* in the first place.

So, how do we find access to our deepest, truly authentic desires? More importantly, how do we actually bring our goals alive, into our reality, into manifestation? Different cultures, different paths, offer us various approaches to finding and manifesting our authentic desires. Almost all of them have in common that we really have to put ourselves up to our elbows into the "mud" of our patterns, habits, beliefs, emotions and inner blockades if we really want to get ahead.

It seems obvious that this usually isn't a pleasant process. It is not for nothing that in Ho'oponopono—the Hawaiian way of inner peace, which I have had the good fortune to get to know intensively in recent years—tears are sometimes called God's "irrigation system" for inner development. However, this practice book, which is based on an audio course I created some time ago for publication on Insight Timer, one of the world's most widespread meditation apps, is about a more relaxed form of how we can trace our authentic desires and objectives and support their manifestation in our lives: the *sankalpa*.

With a sankalpa—sometimes also called *heart's desire*—we plant a seed into our subconscious during meditation, which then supports the realization of our objective from within. This usually helps things develop much more fluidly, effortlessly and with more speed. Are you interested in hearing more about that? All right, let's dive in.

ANDREAS ZIÖRJEN

2 HOW DO WISHES ARISE?

Every day we make thousands of decisions. Many, even most, of them are simple, often subconscious repetitions of earlier decisions. We only very rarely decide out of a real, conscious, authentic desire. As well, the achievement of the objectives that we consciously want to achieve in our lives is often hindered by these same subconscious imprints and subconsciously triggered repetitions of past decisions. A sankalpa is like a seed that anchors our conscious intentions also on this level, and thus, beats blocking subconscious patterns "with their own weapons."

Every day of our lives, we make thousands of more or less conscious decisions about how to go on: small decisions, such as which trousers to wear today, big decisions, such as whether we want to have children or not. Many of them have already become such a habit for us that we rarely even recognize them as decisions that have to be made again and again. For example, you won't remind yourself every morning that you might choose not to go to work, dress differently than usual or wish the honking driver behind you a good morning instead of getting upset.

That's also a good thing, of course. If we had to think every single decision through, repeatedly, we would be hopelessly overwhelmed. Ultimately, however, we make all our decisions for one of three reasons:

a) because of a conscious wish for ourselves or others

   ("I want to reach a goal"),

b) due to subconscious conditioning

   ("everybody just does it that way"), or

6

c)   out of habit ("I've always done it this way").

Then, there are also decisions that we want to make consciously but are still unable to implement. Think, for example, of the smoker who wants to quit but always starts smoking again, of the manager who realizes that his job is no longer healthy for him and the people around him, but who is afraid of the consequences of quitting, of the meditator who believes that her daily meditation brings valuable insights and still can never regularly fit it into her daily routine. I am sure you too know such examples from your own experience.

What hinders us in the pursuit of such objectives, the realization of which would often undoubtedly have positive consequences for us? You may already have guessed: what hinders us are our subconscious habits, beliefs and conditioning.

There are many ways modern spirituality offers us to resolve subconscious blockages. *Sankalpa* is one of those possibilities. It is one that has been used for centuries in the tradition of tantric yoga and is characterized by special simplicity. Often also called "heart's desire," it can help us in achieving almost all objectives we may think of in our lives. A sankalpa is an order passed by our naturally limited judgment directed at the subconscious mind. Therefore, it should be chosen with great care, as once the subconscious has understood this order, its concrete form of realization largely bypasses our conscious influence.

For such an expression of will to have the intended, maximally positive effect for you and your environment, this exercise book gives you the tools to recognize your authentic needs in the first place, and then to state your intentions correctly. You can use those tools not only to create one "great" sankalpa—the heart's desire—but also more generally as an aid to the manifestation of almost all the desires and objectives that you pursue in your life.

Before we dive into the first meditation exercise of this book, I would like to share one more thought with you, right at the beginning, which we will consider more profoundly in the following chapters. Actually, all wishes and objectives are only *vikalpa*. In yoga, this is what we call all concepts, ideas and projections that do not have an independent reality. We find perfection in the present moment only, and the present moment *cannot and does not need to be improved*.

Thus, an excessive focus on not yet manifested objectives tends to divert us from our true core rather than bringing us closer to it—therefore, not really being in line with yoga's primary goal, which is inner liberation. However, as I already mentioned at the beginning, because we *must* continually make decisions and *must* act as a condition of our being, working with the sankalpa is merely a way to make our actions freer, more loving and more helpful for ourselves and others, therefore, also potentially helping us in sustaining our yoga or meditation practice. Let us keep this in mind as we continue to explore the manifestation power of our will.

EXERCISE 1: *NAMASTE* MEDITATION

In the first exercise, we connect with our inmost, Divine nature. The well-known Indian greeting *namaste* (emphasis on the "e," pronounced like an "a" as in "nature") means this exactly: I recognize the Absolute in myself and everyone and everything I encounter inside and outside of myself.

Set a timer for ten minutes or another period that is appropriate for you at this moment.

Sit down with your spine as upright as possible. Make sure that the soles of your feet keep good contact with the ground. Now, close your eyes. Relax your hip joints, shoulders and jaw.

Start to repeat the mantra "namaste" silently inside of yourself. Namaste. Namaste. Namaste. Namaste... Repeat the mantra until your timer indicates the end of the meditation. This type of practice is called *mantra japa* in Indian traditions.

To end this meditation, slowly release the mantra. Be aware of your body. During this day, try again and again to imagine that everything and everyone you encounter is the expression of a perfect universe. With certain things, it will be easier for you to do this than with others. Observe this, too. Try to judge yourself and others as little as possible.

CLARIFYING QUESTIONS ON CHAPTER 2

For each chapter, you will find some clarifying questions that are designed to help you to understand yourself better as well as integrate the contents of the book. The suggested answer options are by no means covering all possibilities but can give you further thought impulses.

What is your relationship to your wishes?

Completely happy, no desires. / Wonderful if they come true, but if they don't, no matter. / When I wish for something, I do everything I can for my wish to come true. / I don't believe in dreams. I have been disappointed too often.

You recognize within yourself a wish the realization of which does not seem very realistic. How do you react?

Interesting. What could this wish tell me about myself? / I shouldn't have this wish. It just makes everything more difficult. / Impossible? There is no such thing, but is it really worth the effort? / Well, let's do it. Pursuing this wish will be a great experience for sure!

Do you have projects that you have wanted to tackle for a long time, but you stand in your own way or the circumstances seem to be against you?

Yes, many. / Rather few. I do most of what I really want. / I never really thought about it. / I don't have time for any new projects.

3 GET WHAT WE WANT—AND WANT WHAT WE HAVE…

If we do not fully accept the here-and-now, paradoxically, this hampers us in manifesting a future for ourselves that is different from our present situation. Non-acceptance binds vast amounts of energy that we could use for different purposes. As we begin to scrutinize our authentic needs and formulate our objectives more concretely, this kind of acceptance frees us to truly recognize our deeper desires and not just act out of learned patterns.

ANDREAS ZIÖRJEN

In Chapter 2, we have seen how our decisions come to be and that many parts in this process take place in the subconscious. In fact, our decisions are so heavily dependent on subconscious factors that many philosophers and scientists even completely doubt the existence of a free will. We will have a closer look at that in the next chapter.

Here, I would like first to introduce another idea that is central to the effect of the *sankalpa*: the acceptance and love of the here-and-now. All our strength lies in the here-and-now. If we do not accept what is now, our present situation, we are losing a great deal of energy.

Now, of course, you might object that a sankalpa is an objective as well, something that is not yet present in our lives at the moment. Otherwise, the whole thing would be pointless. Classical common sense seems to indicate that we must be unhappy about what is to move away from it. That is, we are taught to fear. We think we would not even be

16

motivated at all to move away from the present point of our life or to improve if we managed to feel fully comfortable in the present moment. This truly is a common, even if unnecessary, belief pattern. One of the most visible forms it takes is when we feel— undoubtedly also due to our educational system—that we need to improve and optimize ourselves continually. We can even walk into this trap when we define our sankalpa.

I would like to suggest a somewhat different way to look at the improvement of self and outer circumstances: in yoga, we assume that we are always in the right place at the right time and that we don't need to gain anything to be perfect and complete. However, as a condition of our existence, we must continually keep deciding and acting on our decisions, as we saw in the last Chapter.

This means that we are also always *moving*. Our decision to repeat yesterday's decision, and therefore, allow things to continue as they are is *also a new decision*, although then everything superficially remains the same. Sankalpa is about consciously steering in

17

the direction we want to go—because we cannot stand still, we can just choose either to let go of the wheel and close our eyes or not.

However, if we do not really accept where we stand right now, then it is as if we were walking on the spot; we are only losing energy that we could actually use for our progress. Aside from this, our subconscious is also pretty smart: it knows very well that we won't really feel comfortable, even after reaching our goal, if we are already negative about where we are now. Therefore, paradoxically, full acceptance of the present situation *helps us to change things*—and increases the effect of our sankalpa many times over.

EXERCISE 2: MIRROR WORK

For today's exercise, I recommend that you stand in front of a mirror or use a hand mirror. If this is not possible, you can also just imagine talking to your mirror image.

Stand or sit in front of your mirror. Set your meditation timer to five minutes or any other duration that suits you. Look yourself in the eyes and smile at yourself. Tell yourself, in your head, or if possible, aloud and clearly: *I now choose to love myself and my world unconditionally. I now choose to love myself and my world unconditionally.* Repeat this sentence for the duration of the meditation, all the while keeping eye contact with your reflection. If this exercise should turn out to be difficult for you or trigger unpleasantly strong emotions, you can close your eyes at any time and just concentrate on breathing until the timer chimes.

At the end of the time, maintain eye contact for one more moment and fall silent again. Smile at yourself once more, then close your eyes. Perceive the body in its entirety. How do you feel now? During this day, try to turn your attention to your mirror image whenever you see it somewhere and say to yourself: *I thank you for my being.* If you should happen to be an advanced practitioner in such exercises, you might also try to do this meditation again with a human counterpart.

IN-DEPTH QUESTIONS ON CHAPTER 3

On a scale of 1 to 10, how happy do you feel right now?

1-3 / 4-6 / 6-9 / 10

On a scale of 1 to 10, how happy are you with your life in general?

1-3 / 4-6 / 6-9 / 10

How easy or difficult was it for you to look in your mirror image's eyes?

Pleasant / Unpleasant / Difficult / Other (what?)

4 WHAT IS FREE WILL, REALLY?

Among philosophers, and in yoga, it is controversial whether free will is only a useful concept or a reality. Regardless of this, we must *act as if we had a choice because deciding—or having the impression of deciding—is a fundamental condition of our lives. In any case, our decisions are determined by memories and subconscious imprints to a much larger extent than we usually realize. So, how do we distinguish between objectives that actually help us to move forward and objectives that are not really "ours?"*

Philosopher Arthur Schopenhauer is known for stating: "Man can do what he wills, but he cannot will what he wills." In the last chapter, we saw that unconditionally accepting our present situation helps us in moving towards our goals. How do we set these objectives in the first place? How do we know what we want? How can we decide whether to accept our current situation? Modern brain research has shown that all our decisions and actions can already be measured in the brain even before we can consciously perceive the need for a decision and make it! So, is there—as many philosophers and scientists assume today—no free will at all?

It is indisputable that, in our everyday life, we feel as if we can influence the course of events by our conscious decisions. In the second chapter, we stated that we cannot *not act* at all, so that the decision to do nothing is a kind of decision too, and thus, an action. We are continually making decisions as long as we live, whether we want to or not. Therefore, free will is a kind of working hypothesis of our existence, a part of our experience. It is well known that in hatha yoga, as a science of experience, we work directly with our directly experienceable reality, be it the body or our other sensory perceptions.

If all of this sounds a bit theoretical to you, don't worry. This is not a philosophy book, but a practical exercise set designed to help you fulfill your deepest desires. In the next chapter, we will discuss how exactly we go about this. However, to be able to define your objectives "correctly," we do need a basic understanding of how our desires actually come about, what a real desire is and how we distinguish it from objectives that we have taken on from outside and of which we only believe that they correspond to our own needs. So, let's stay with the theory for one more moment.

To summarize, a wish is a kind of decision or evaluation: we prefer an event on our path of life—the fulfillment of a wish—over all of those scenarios in which the wish is not fulfilled.

In Chapter 2, we have seen that decisions can be triggered by three fundamental kinds of impulses: Either we want to achieve a goal (i.e., fulfill a wish), or we decide out of habit or from unconscious conditioning. However, we have just discovered that all of our desires—the first kind of trigger—are also a kind of decision. This means that every wish can be caused by one of the three reasons described above again, two of them being born out of conditioning. If we find out again that there is no conditioning behind the first wish, but a "real" wish, we could theoretically go on like this indefinitely.

By the way, do you remember the old joke about the teacher asking a little girl: "What's holding up the earth?" When she replies "a giant turtle carries it on its back," he shrewdly asks: "What is the turtle standing on, then?" The answer is: "Oh, you're just trying to confuse me. It's obviously turtles all the way down!"

Going back to our example, that, in turn, means that somewhere we need a beginning, a creation of this chain of decisions if we don't want to end up with nothing but conditioning. That is then either the free will or, for those who do not believe in it, it's merely our unconscious patterns at the root of all our behavior when the probability for any wish to have been original has become infinitely small.

Regardless of which option you choose to believe in yourself, it has become clear from this example that each of our actions and desires is probably primarily determined by our learned patterns, habits and conditioning.

Now, we come to the heart of the matter: this conclusion means, if we think it through to the end, that most of our desires are not actually "our desires," but fragments from the past and adopted ideas— from teachers, parents, friends or society as a whole.

This conditioning and these memories are predominantly mental imprints in our minds and are controlled by memories of some kind. What I would like to call "authentic" desires, on the other hand, arises *here and now*, out of a creative impulse much more in tune with the flow of life than our relatively static conditionings. Therefore, it is critical that we learn to pay attention to our higher intuition and our physical sensations when making our decisions because those aspects of our subconscious—let's call them the "light" aspects—know very well what really works for us, and what does not. They cannot be duped by purely mental constructs.

Personally, I am convinced that we do have free will, at least on the very practical level of our seemingly independent existence. However, I also believe that if we don't practice it over and over again, we all use it very rarely—too rarely. Most of us—and this goes for me, too—, we spend a large part of our lives living on autopilot. Yoga and meditation may help us to remain aware, conscious and present during more and more of our time here in this world. This is crucial, for it is in the here-and-now that we find the impulse of free will—our ability to say "no" to things that do not correspond to our highest and most loving state of being.

EXERCISE 3: ALLOWING THE BREATH TO FLOW

Sit and straighten your spine as best you can. Set your timer to a period of between ten and twenty minutes. Close your eyes. Observe carefully how your body is touching your seat or the ground. Then, train your attention on your breathing. Allow your breathing to flow as freely as possible. Whenever you notice that you are somehow deliberately influencing your breathing, resolve to release that impulse immediately. If you wish, you can stay with this and simply continue to observe yourself breathing. However, if that feels good, you may now add counting your exhalations from one to ten. When you have reached ten, start again from one. Do not influence the breathing; this remains the primary focus.

After the time has elapsed, gently let go of the exercise and continue breathing freely. On this day, pay particular attention to your wishes and from where they arise. Just observe them as precisely as you can, as consistently as possible. To support this, you can repeat the following phrase from time to time during your day: I pay attention to my true needs.

Now, move your fingers and toes, arms and legs, stretch your whole body. Then, open your eyes and return to your daily life.

CLARIFYING QUESTIONS ON CHAPTER 4

Do you think you have free will?

Yes / No / Maybe sometimes / Don't know

In which of the following four areas do you currently see the most need for development in your life?

Profession, vocation and finances / Relationships / Self-love / Health

5 VISUALIZING THE OUTCOME

When we create a sankalpa, it is essential that we choose a desire that really helps us in our personal development, as well as meeting one or several of our most profound needs. It is not for nothing that sankalpa is sometimes called the heart's desire. To recognize whether we have chosen our objective with our heart and not just our head and whether our whole being really wants this or not, we work with the technique of the positive outcome visualization.

In the last three chapters, we have found that

both our desires and our actions to fulfill them are not only determined by the conscious part of ourselves. If we admit that as truth, this also means that our objectives are a result of our free will only to a very limited extent. However, we have also realized that yoga and meditation help us to gain more and more clarity about our true needs beyond old patterns and conditioning.

Man is a being of thought, of concepts. In this and the next chapter, we will discuss how we can use the analytical abilities of our minds to help us consciously formulate desires that come from the most profound depths of our soul. To find out if these desires are true or just mental ideals constructed from old beliefs and outdated patterns of thought, we test them with our emotions.

To do this, we use the instrument called *positive outcome visualization*, which is also used in various areas of psychology and shamanic manifestation techniques. Let's give it a try right away:

Think of something you wish to experience, achieve or have more of in your life. If you can't think of anything significant at the moment, you can also imagine what you would like to have for lunch today. Ready? Keep your attention trained on your feelings throughout the following exercise. If something doesn't feel absolutely and unquestionably good, change something about the situation in your inner picture until it feels as comfortable as possible.

Now, imagine yourself as you would be in the situation in which this wish has already been fulfilled. Imagine what you'd look like, what you can see around you. How does your environment smell? Is there a taste that you can associate with the situation? What does the situation sound like? What do you say? What do the people around you say? Are there touches or physical sensations? For example, if you want to go on a vacation at the seaside, you might imagine the touch of the warm salt water on your skin when snorkeling at the beach. Bring as many details as possible into your imagination. If you could now describe your feeling, what words would you use? … Stay with this image for a moment.

Well, what was that like? Maybe it was easy for you to find a positive emotion. Maybe doubts or thoughts arose during this visualization, for example, "but actually this has disadvantages, too," or "this is too good to be true." Perhaps it was even difficult to imagine the situation at all. Especially with chronic illnesses, or after long-lasting injuries, it sometimes happens that we can no longer even imagine being completely healthy.

Luckily, a sankalpa can also help in such cases and "weaken" the old imprints telling our subconscious that we're—for example—irreparably damaged in some way. This is a very good thing since this kind of subconscious imprint can very strongly hinder our natural healing processes. When defining a sankalpa, it is only important to find a final image that feels unreservedly positive, even if details may still be difficult to visualize at the beginning or if there are doubts about its feasibility.

If this should be the case and you experience

difficulty visualizing the positive outcome, make yourself aware that this is only an idea. In our imagination, anything is possible, and you may take the liberty of feeling what it would be like, just to see. However, if the outcome you imagined itself does not feel absolutely bright and positive for you, continue to change it until that is the case. A feeling that is not absolutely pleasant would be an indication that your desire is guided by inner conditioning.

Come back to your positive outcome imagination from the exercise we just did. If one represents the maximum distance from this situation and ten represents the situation already being present in your life, in reality, where on the scale would you be now? If you're not at ten (which I assume, otherwise you needn't imagine the outcome), what are the hindrances preventing you from being at ten now? Are there internal or external things that you would have to let go of to get there? Would you now be ready to let go of these things? Are there things you'd need to do? Are you willing to do these things?

In yoga, we call this kind of practice *svadhyaya*,

self-analysis. The last point, letting go, is of central importance for the effectiveness of any manifestation technique. We don't just need to be willing to let go of the obstacles that we may have already grown fond of, but that still separate us from the goal. Ultimately, we must also let go of the urgency and absoluteness of wanting to reach this objective. Of course, we want to do everything we can to make it happen—but we should not try to steer our fate with all our might.

The advantage of the sankalpa method is that we only define our objective and then place the choice of the exact path to reach it into the hands of our subconscious. We only play along. We no longer steer as forcefully with our intellect as we might have learned. To loosen our grip a bit and get away from "trying so hard," I have found the following considerations to be of help for many practitioners:

Imagine the worst thing that could happen if your wish were not fulfilled or if even the opposite were to happen. What would happen? How likely is it that this will actually occur and that the wish will not manifest itself at all to any degree or in any form? Often, there are many possible outcomes between best case and worst case. What skills would you need to deal with the worst-case scenario? Do you have these skills?

Remaining aware that life almost always goes on without great restrictions, even if our wishes are not fulfilled, helps us to let go. Paradoxically, letting go actually helps us to fulfill our desires. Of course, letting go does not mean, for example, not to learn before an exam or not to study realty advertisements when you are looking for a new house. Everything depends on whether we are doing this in a compulsive way or with an open attitude.

EXERCISE 4: THE LIST OF OBJECTIVES

For this exercise, you will need a sheet of paper and a pen. You may also use the template on the next page to get started.

Sit with your spine upright but flexible. Meditation postures should never be rigid and allow for movement. If possible, make sure that you can write without leaving the posture. Close your eyes for a moment and turn your attention inward. Observe the flow of your breathing.

Now, open your eyes and name the sheet of paper in front of you "My objectives." Start with point one. In a short, condensed phrase, write down a personal goal, an objective that you would like to achieve for yourself at this moment in life. That might be anything, big or small, important or unimportant from buying a new pair of trousers tomorrow to establishing a daily meditation practice, from writing a book to really loving yourself or being financially independent. Really anything, whatever comes up first. Be spontaneous, think as little as possible and try not to judge yourself. Then, continue with point two. Always come back to observing your breathing. How is its flow? When you finished point two, continue and add as many objectives as possible to your list. Try to find at least ten objectives in total, the more, the better.

When you feel nothing more will come at the moment (or when the time you allotted yourself for this exercise runs out, of course), put the pen aside. Close your eyes and monitor your breathing. Be as present as possible. Observe your breathing and your thoughts without interfering. How are you feeling right now?

After some time, direct your senses outward again. Keep the list with you today and complete it if you can think of anything else. You will need the list again for the exercise in the next chapter. There, we will work with needs and strategies and discuss how a good sankalpa can be created based on our desires and objectives.

SANKALPA

MY LIST OF OBJECTIVES

Date: 11/1/19

stability 1. financial independence

security 2. Self-forgiveness

3. healthy relationships

thrive 4. healthy relationship w/environment

5. action w/ intention and purpose

6. _____

7. _____

8. _____

9. _____

10. _____

43

CLARIFYING QUESTIONS ON CHAPTER 5

How often do you think about what you want to achieve in your life?

Daily. / Several times a month. / Less often. / Actually, never consciously.

How many objectives have you noted on your objectives list?

Just one big one, I got stuck with that. / Several, but I'm not at ten yet. / Ten, but I had to think quite a bit to find them. / Ten or more.

If you look at your list of objectives, how do you feel about it now?

Wonderful, so many beautiful things are still coming towards me. Let's go for it! / That won't work anyway. / OMG, so much to do! / Nice objectives, but actually my life is already great just the way it is.

6 NEEDS AND STRATEGIES

We've seen that a sankalpa *is supposed to be about something very fundamental.* Needs *are the fundamental driving forces behind everything we do and want to do. In this chapter, we'll have a look at what needs are about and what role they play in formulating a sankalpa or any other objectives we can think of. By considering our needs while defining what we truly want, we can better ensure that we do not produce undesirable or counterproductive results with the sankalpa technique, because—obviously—we cannot think of everything in advance.*

In the last chapter, we were asking ourselves about our objectives and desires for ourselves in life. By now, we also already know how we can see whether these objectives really correspond to our innermost, authentic desires: for this, again, we can use positive outcome visualization and continue refining our perception and emotional awareness. Often, making the "right" wishes isn't easy. Just think of the people who always believe they are choosing the seemingly "right" lovers in life, and yet, their relationships do not last as long as they desire.

The positive outcome visualization gives us a first indication of what might have gone wrong in such cases: When we use this instrument, we focus above all on how the situation should *feel* for us once the desire has been fulfilled. This means that we look for what *feeling*, what emotions, the best possible result we would like to produce for ourselves. In the example of the search for a suitable partner, this means that we focus less on how he or she should be exactly, but rather on how a really optimal relationship will feel for us, what experiences we would like to make in that area of our lives.

So, in what way precisely this "best possible result" will manifest in our lives, we leave as open as possible, so that we can be sidetracked or sabotaged as little as possible by our innermost saboteurs—our thoughts and behavior patterns.

To understand this even better, allow me a small detour into the science of communication.

Starting in the 1960s, American psychologist Marshall B. Rosenberg intensively researched the ways destructive conflicts arise and can be avoided, or maybe better put, resolved more constructively and humanely. One of his conclusions was that we often do not communicate our real needs to the other when we have a desire, but already have a particular strategy in mind about how exactly we would like this to be fulfilled. Perhaps we are often not even aware that the strategy we want the other to "play along with" is not really a need.

Let me give an example: You walk through town and feel like a chocolate ice cream. There may be all kinds of needs behind this desire. Maybe you're just hungry. Maybe you want to *distract* yourself from something. Then, the need might instead be something like *inner peace.* Maybe it's hot, and you want to cool down to meet your need for *physical well-being.* Whatever it may be, ice cream is a strategy, and we could meet each of these needs differently. When it comes to cooling down, for example, a sip of cool spring water (or technically, even a cup of warm mint tea) might be more effective.

A pretty good indicator that we are talking about a need is that it can only be positive and that it is only about ourselves. On the other hand, our *strategies* for meeting specific needs are usually determined by our patterns and beliefs and may even harm ourselves and others if they are not appropriate for the situation at hand.

Why is this important to us? When formulating our objectives and the sankalpa, we should start on as basic a level as possible (i.e., we should use them to address our true, most essential needs). Let us go back to the interesting example of the search for a partner one more moment. Although this will not be the usual topic for a sankalpa, some basic principles can be very well illustrated with this. Aside from this, we almost all know this from some time or another in our lives. We will look at the more spiritual uses for desire manifestation in the next chapters.

So, let's say you have a crush on your attractive neighbor. It might be obvious, then, to set yourself the objective of getting together with this person, at least if you are both single. There's nothing wrong with that. However, if we want to consciously ask the help of our subconscious, for example, with a sankalpa or by including this desire on the list of objectives we started in the last chapter, then we should definitely move a little more cautiously to avoid undesirable side effects and to remain energetically and ethically sound.

First of all, a good sankalpa should always about yourself only and not any other conscious being because as soon as you try to intervene into the will of other beings directly or indirectly using your will, energetically strange and rather unpleasant side effects may arise, since the conscious or unconscious objectives of the other being are perhaps entirely different from yours.

From a purely ethical point of view, this is a smaller problem than you might think. This is because all of the processes stimulated by sankalpa take place between your subconscious and the subconscious of the other being and are, therefore, automatically moving in line with the broader needs of both of you. So, you can't use this technique to influence others to their disadvantage, and therefore, you can't harm them unintentionally either.

However, the attempt to influence other beings, no matter if you think you mean well, *will* build tension within yourself. Then, at some point, this tension will dissolve into unpleasant vibrations— namely when you have built up this subconscious willpower on your side, but it does not find resonance with the other. This even applies if the other person explicitly says they want the same thing as you do—

because they're certainly not one hundred percent aware of their soul plan either. So, a sankalpa should be addressed *at ourselves exclusively*.

Another point to consider is this: your desire for a relationship with your neighbor again is only a strategy for fulfilling a need. This seems obvious for most of us in this case. In more complicated situations, we can easily determine whether our desire is based on a need or a strategy by asking ourselves what we really want to get out of it. In this case, for example, this might be something like *giving and receiving love*, satisfying our need for *intimacy* or *companionship*, *sexual fulfillment* or any number of other factors.

So, to conclude this train of thought, assuming we'd want to use *sankalpa* to resolve this situation, we won't state that we want to be with the other person. Instead, we have several possibilities to support our conscious intention through sankalpa or the list of objectives:

a) We take a closer look at the positive outcome visualization of our project, considering it as impartially as possible. What is it that really constitutes the positive effect of our wish coming true for us? What kind of emotions do we want to arise? How can we formulate our objectives in such a way that our experience stands in the foreground? The way you might put our example in your list of objectives might then be something like: *I live a wonderful and lasting relationship with a loving, attractive and suitable partner.* You might even add mentally that you'd just love your attractive neighbor to be that partner. However, it is vital that you leave that particular point open in your formulation because we don't really know whether this exact person can really fulfill our wish. Only our own subconscious and that of the other person know that.

b) We think about the needs behind the desire for a relationship with this person. For example, *being loved* or *intimacy*. Take care not to include negations. "Not being alone" for example wouldn't constitute a need, for it draws your attention on what you want to avoid instead on what you want to achieve. Once we understand our needs in this matter, we formulate our objective as generally as possible based on that understanding. The formulation in the list might then be, for example, *I am always completely loved by myself, other people and the Divine, and I express this in my relationships every day.*

c) We think about how we would need to be ourselves to fit optimally into this positive final image, and focus our objectives on it. An example of this: *I am completely ready for a mutually fulfilling love relationship with a loving and perfectly fitting person.* In principle, you could even insert the neighbor here, since it's only about your side of the subject. Personally, however, I would advise you not to do this, as it would close your mind to others and perhaps other possibilities even more in harmony with the "big picture".

Perhaps you can already see that these principles can be applied to almost everything we want to achieve in life. Be it passing an exam, a new job, spiritual awakening, finding our calling or planning a pleasant journey for our vacation, we just have to do it.

EXERCISE 5: IDENTIFYING NEEDS

This exercise is about actively working with your desires. Take your list of objectives and look at it for a moment. Close your eyes, straighten up and observe your breathing for a few moments. Relax your hip area, your belly, shoulders and jaw.

Now, open your eyes and turn to the list. Reread it once more, applying your newfound knowledge about needs and strategies. If you find an item on the list to be a strategy, write the needs you want to have fulfilled through it in brackets behind or below the entry. Again, needs are always positive. They represent the most profound inner benefit we hope to gain from achieving the objective.

Take a break now, no matter how far you've come. Look again at the needs you have just written. Maybe some of them will repeat themselves on several points. If so, after this exercise you may want to add points that clearly address those needs to your list of objectives.

Then, close your eyes again. Set your timer to an appropriate time, allow the following sentence to emerge from within, and start repeating it in your mind: *I am firmly anchored in love and joy.*

When the timer chimes, let go of the mantra. Perceive the whole body and your free-flowing breath. Rub your palms against each other and put them on your eyes for a moment. Drop them again, move your body and stretch softly. Open your eyes. Repeat once more in a conscious state this exercise's key phrase: *I am firmly anchored in love and joy.* You can also repeat it from time to time during the day. If you like this kind of work, consider continuing to work on your list of objectives today.

CLARIFYING QUESTIONS ON CHAPTER 6

If you are already meditating, what do you think is your primary motivation for it?

Improve quality of life (e.g., calmness, relaxation) /

Spiritual development and inner freedom /

Improving your health / Do not know / Other

Which one of the following needs seems to be most important to you at the moment?

Self-determination / Security / Self-development / Contribution

Which of the following strategies for fulfilling needs have you experienced most frequently in your life (in yourself or others?)?

Cooperation and teamwork / Manipulation and control / Asking politely / Premature obedience

7 GRATITUDE AND LETTING GO

Gratitude and letting go are two sides of the same coin and can greatly increase the effectiveness of a sankalpa. If we cultivate gratitude as a basic attitude in our lives, we create a lush garden in the subconscious in which the seed of our sankalpa can germinate and grow. We can practice this. In this chapter, we will learn how to cultivate the emotion of gratitude and how to see events in our lives from different angles.

In Chapter 6, we have considered the nature of needs and strategies, and we have seen how we can approach the formulation of objectives and sankalpas. A good sankalpa should always be determined more by our needs than our strategies to fulfill them, at least as far as possible. Needs, as we've seen, are essential and exclusively positive. On the other hand, strategies always aim to fulfill a need, but are interchangeable and can also take on less helpful forms. They can even hurt us or others if they are coming out of old, possibly destructive, thought patterns.

In this chapter, we will take on the topic of gratitude and letting go. If you manage to cultivate gratitude as a basic attitude in your life, fertile soil will develop in the garden of your subconscious, where the seed of your sankalpa has optimal conditions to germinate and get taller. We can practice this. To really live in gratitude is not only to appreciate the obvious, good and positive things in our lives. It also means looking at more complex situations that we will unavoidably encounter on our way at one time or another from different angles, and acknowledging its positive aspects—but without denying their difficult or unpleasant aspects.

This practice—sometimes also called *cognitive reframing*—helps us to look at the challenges in our lives from a bird's eye view, and to cope better with them. We must let go of our natural tendency to cling to the negative aspects of our challenges and of allowing our thoughts to revolve around them. If we make a habit of consciously cultivating gratitude, this will become easier and easier over time.

EXERCISE 6: GRATITUDE AND APPRECIATION

Sit comfortably in your meditation posture and set your meditation timer to a time between fifteen and twenty-five minutes, divided by two intermediate bells. Your meditation will contain three separate parts of more or less equal length.

Close your eyes and take one deep breath. Be mindful of your present state. How do you feel at this moment? Linger a moment with this feeling. Then, concentrate on the wide-open space in front of your closed eyes. Keeping your awareness there, ask yourself the following question: *What am I grateful for?* Observe what appears within yourself to answer this question. It may be a word, a picture or a spontaneous thought. Let the answer have its effect on you for a moment, then ask again: What am I grateful for? Continue doing this for a while....

At the end of the first third of the exercise, let

go of the question again. Allow your breathing to flow freely and naturally. How are you feeling now?

Now, invoke a situation in front of your inner eye that was difficult for you in the past. Look at your memories of it for a moment. However small it may be, is there anything there that you can be grateful for? For example, something like how you dealt with the challenge at that time, what you have learned out of it, or any positive aspects later in your life that you probably would not have experienced without this difficult situation occurring first? It is not about denying or trivializing the difficulty and/or negativity of the situation. In this exercise, we want to recognize that our judgments and evaluations usually focus only on a part of the actual event with all its effects. Stay with this for a moment; observe the situation and its effects on your life as neutrally as possible from all sides.

When the second intermediate bell sounds, release yourself from this exercise too, and linger in your inner space. Take in the following sentence and repeat it to yourself during the third part of the exercise, very attentively and presently: *"Thank you for my being."*

After the whole meditation time has elapsed, please breathe out deeply once, and then breathe in again. Open your eyes. Repeat once more in this conscious state and, if possible, in a loud voice: *Thank you for my being.* Take this sentence with you throughout your day and return to it from time to time. If you pass a mirror some time, you can also look into your own eyes and thank yourself for your being. This will further intensify the effect of the exercise.

Now, take another look at your list of objectives. Rate each of the objectives on a scale from one to nine to see how close you have come to achieving them.

One means: I currently have no means and ability ever to achieve this objective, and have not yet taken any steps to acquire these means and abilities. Nine means you are almost there and there is very little left. Most of your objectives will be somewhere in between. How grateful can you be for what you have already achieved?

CLARIFYING QUESTIONS ON CHAPTER 7

What are you most grateful for, right now?

to be here at all / to have enough to eat every day / to live in relative freedom / a television program / something else (what?)

How often do you consciously feel gratitude in your everyday life?

several times a day / almost always / daily / not daily, but often / less often

ॐ

8 CREATING A SANKALPA

In this chapter, we review the basics and have a closer look at the rules for formulating an effective sankalpa or objective. In the meditation at the end, you will receive examples of formulations and learn how to find your own space to let your topic rise.

In Chapter 7, we discussed the role of gratitude as a foundation as well as an enhancer for effectiveness for our sankalpa. In this chapter, we get to the heart of the matter and put together the basics learned in the last chapters. So, let us take a look at how a sankalpa is found in detail and what exactly we can do with it. As I mentioned at the beginning of this book, sankalpa means higher intention or resolve. It is something like the essence of our path and aspiration. We resolve to keep it for a long time— since, like a planted sequoia seed in our garden, it also needs a certain amount of care and attention to grow. Therefore, it should be chosen and formulated with care.

The following *principles for formulating intentions* may also be used for less basic formulations of objectives than just a "real" sankalpa. That is why we are again using everyday examples here for clarity.

First:

Be brief and concise; limit yourself to a single, short phrase. Make sure that you leave the wording exactly the same whenever you repeat it. This helps the subconscious to anchor the intention more profoundly.

Second:

Formulate a sankalpa whenever possible in the present tense. So, for example, we don't say "I *will* become spiritually and materially rich" but "I *am* spiritually and materially rich."

Third:

A sankalpa should not contain any "negative" words, nor negations in the formulation or even as part of the words you use, and should trigger a clear, exclusively good feeling. So, for example, we do not say: "I have no more pain" or "I am painless," but rather something like: "Well-being, lightness and health penetrate every cell of my being."

Fourth:

Focus more on your being, on your state of existence, than on doing or having. Keep the need that you want to fulfill in the foreground, not the strategy. So, think about what you will be like when your heart's desire is fulfilled, how it will feel. The tool of the positive outcome visualization from Chapter 5 will help you to do this. So, for example, we won't say: "I will successfully complete my training as a therapist (or anything else)," but rather something like "I am an excellent therapist and bring my light into the world through my abilities."

Fifth:

Keep other beings out of your sankalpa, and only take responsibility for your own being. We have already talked about this. So, we don't say for example: "My dog and I always get along splendidly," but rather "I am a wonderful and loving friend and caretaker for my dog."

Sixth:

Think carefully about what you would have to let

70

go so that your sankalpa can fulfill itself, and whether you are really prepared to do something for its realization. The sankalpa will always take you in the direction you desire, making you more open to new opportunities, but it can, of course, be unpleasant if you set yourself an objective that you have trouble accepting the consequences and side effects of when it's coming true. If you have conditions, you should ideally include them explicitly in the sankalpa. Otherwise, you cannot expect them to be met. To use the example of partnership again: Let us assume that you live in a relationship that does you no good, but you do not want to let go of your partner under any circumstances. You recognize the problem and want to change something. You choose the absolutely valid sankalpa *"I only live joyful, nourishing and light relationships"* in the hope that your existing relationship will change in this way. This may happen if the other side is ready for this development too, but it may also happen that strong dividing currents occur because the resonance of your partner no longer corresponds to your new inner alignment. Here, we can also see the limits of the sankalpa method: due to the fifth basic rule, you cannot include other people, because that would be an act of violence.

EXERCISE 7: FINDING YOUR SANKALPA

In today's meditation, we will look at some possible forms of sankalpas in the significant areas of human life experience, then open a space to allow your own impulses to arise. Even more suggestions for sankalpa formulations may be found in the last chapter of this book and, for example, in the guided sankalpa meditations available at www.chakra-atelier.ch, the shortest of which can be heard free of charge on *Insight Timer*.

These main areas are:

- basic trust and security (root chakra),
- relationship (sacral chakra),
- profession and vocation (solar plexus chakra),
- healing and love (heart chakra),
- authenticity (throat chakra),
- clarity and inner peace (third eye), and

- spirituality (crown chakra).

For this exercise, you will need this book opened in front of you if you do not want to work with a recorded sankalpa meditation. Of course, you may also record this exercise using your own voice. It may be very valuable to listen to your own voice guiding you in meditation. This usually helps you remain even more present than when someone else is guiding you.

Put yourself at ease but still try to sit in an upright meditation posture that is as comfortable as possible for you. The best way to do this is to place the book on a desk and sit on the front edge of a chair before it.

Now, close your eyes for a moment and breathe in and out deeply, but without forcing your breathing. Relax your belly, shoulders, jaw and tongue. Then, open your eyes again and read this text as carefully as possible. Stay aware of your breathing all the time.

Let a picture, a word or a feeling rise spontaneously in your inner space for each of the following words and sentences. Pay attention to which words, ideas or topics you feel a special resonance with.

Garden. Mountain. Ocean. Beach with palm trees. Sun. Wind on a mountain top. Emptiness vibrating with life. Waterfall. Thoughts. Yourself. Joy. Lightness. Love. To be happy. Change. The universe. God. Truth. Power. Courage.

I am free. I am completely myself. I let go of all obstacles. I stand in the fullness of life. I am always connected with Divine inspiration. I am safe. I direct my thoughts towards all that is good and loving. I live the highest expression of my soul. I allow myself to be anything I want to be. I trust in myself and in life. I now choose goodness, love and abundance. I accept my own Divinity. I realize who I really am.

I choose the path of love. I love myself. I am

completely lovable. Courage and self-esteem determine my life. I forgive myself and all others unconditionally. I can take constructive action in any situation and I always give my best. I live in freedom and love, in clarity, insight and joy. I am creative. My life is full of lightness and joy. I am in connection. My vibration becomes higher and higher. I walk the path of love, inside and outside.

I am full of energy and enthusiasm for life. I decide to fulfill all tasks with love, ease and joy. I have the power, the strength and the ability to master everything in life. I am safe in the world of work and live in abundance. I am courageous. I allow myself to be perfect. I recognize and live my vocation, the highest dream of my soul. I let my inner light shine. I am the master of my life. I lovingly live my uniqueness for the good of all being, of the whole. I bless my job with love.

I trust in the best solution for all participants automatically arising. I am safe in the universe, and all being supports me. I live in abundance and in the flow of life. I remain in abundance no matter what I do or where I go. I am always mindful, loving and present with myself and all the beings I meet. I radiate love. I am in harmony with all that is and express this in my actions. I love and accept myself with all my feelings, thoughts, words and actions.

Life loves me, and I am safe. I now choose healthy and fulfilling relationships. My heart is open to love and deeply fulfilling relationships of all kinds. It is safe for me to express love. I am absolutely lovable. It is easy for me to accept love from myself and others. I am complete; I have everything I need. I bless all beings in my life with love. I am firmly anchored in self-love and freedom. I am in harmony with all beings. Wherever I am, there is joy and laughter. I plant new causes of love and peace. I trust my inner voice and am relaxed. I am now totally resting in the love and joy of my humanity.

My body is full of life and vitality. My love cleanses my body and all my cells from negative thoughts about diseases. Full of love, I let go of the past and old beliefs. I plant seeds of love and health in the garden of my life. My love also heals painful memories in my body. Love flows in every cell of my body. I have the power, the strength and the possibility to digest everything that touches me. I am happy, healthy and whole. I am filled with gratitude. I am always connected with the stream of Divine wisdom and life force. Healing love and life energy fill every cell of my body. I open myself to the spiritual flow of healing. I am a channel for the sublime; I am clear and pure. I am completely present.

Peace flows through me, all pressure dissolves.

I now allow the infinite love at the center of my heart to heal everything in me and in my world. Namaste.

Rest in silence and observe your breathing.

………

Recall your intention for this exercise.

....

Prepare to end the exercise. Deepen your breathing.

Open your eyes.

Before you return to your everyday life, take a moment to perceive the effect of the exercise consciously once again. You may want to take some notes. Thank you. I love you, and I love myself.

If you have found an phrase or at least a hint for your sankalpa, please write down your sentence and keep it ready for the meditation of the next chapter.

MY SANKALPA

....

CLARIFYING QUESTIONS ON CHAPTER 8

Have you already found a sankalpa that you can use to start?

Yes. I am already using it. / I have an idea, but it has not yet been formulated. / No. I am still looking for the right topic. / No. I have so many objectives that I can't decide.

Which of the following four sentences appeals most to you at this moment? And why?

- Life nourishes and supports me, I am safe (basic trust).
- I am and remain in abundance no matter where I go and what I do (job and finances).
- Health flows in every cell of my body (health and healing).
- I recognize my Divine core and connect with it (spirituality).

9 APPLYING THE SANKALPA

In this chapter, we will talk about the three most important ways to include your sankalpa in a meditation practice. In the meditation at the end, we plant the seed of your current sankalpa into your inner garden.

Now, I hope you have gained a very good idea of what a sankalpa is and what it can be used for. Perhaps you have already found an initial formulation that can then be further consolidated in your practice. The next two chapters are about how exactly we can integrate our heart's desire into our meditation practice and our everyday life with the greatest possible benefit.

It is actually quite simple: frequency wins over intensity. If your sankalpa is well formulated, in harmony with your innermost needs and desires and well connected with your emotional world, you have already won. Then, it is sufficient merely to repeat it regularly to anchor it deeper and deeper in your experience and ultimately allow it to reach a relatively effortless manifestation. Nevertheless, in meditation, we are particularly close to our core, our subconscious and superconscious. Therefore, repeating your sankalpa in these states has a particularly rapid and good effect.

There are several ways to use your sankalpa in meditation. At this point, I would like to present only the three most important of them:

In the yoga-nidra style I learned, we repeat our sankalpa several times in two places during meditation: The first time after about a quarter of the exercise, after the beginning with the withdrawal of the senses (i.e., as soon as we have attained a certain inner attention), the second time at the end of the exercises in the deeper yoga-nidra state, shortly before the end of the exercise. This can be transferred to any form of meditation. You then repeat the sankalpa as part of, and towards the end of, your entry ritual, and just before the end of the exercise, before you begin to breathe deeper again and move your body.

The second possibility is to use sankalpa as an object of mantra meditation. A sankalpa is ultimately also a *mantra*, a tool of the mind. Throughout the exercise, you concentrate on repeating the sentence and draw attention back to it as soon as your thoughts drift away. Often, it is also helpful to link the repetition of the mantra (called *mantra japa* in the Indian tradition) with natural breathing.

The third possibility is the application of your sankalpa in the context of a visualization. For this, you may create any imaginative setting. Use the one that best suits you; dare to be creative. You might imagine the sankalpa, for example, as a dewdrop falling into the pond of your inner garden (the subconscious) triggering concentric wave circles in it. Alternatively, you imagine the sankalpa as a plant seed, which you cultivate and watch growing.

EXERCISE 8: PLANTING THE SANKALPA

In this exercise, we will look at an example for the third approach we discussed. Sit up straight in your meditation posture. Of course, you can also do any of the meditations of this book lying down if this is more comfortable for you, and you can stay awake (this might possibly be a challenge). Take note of your current state of physical wellbeing, of your feelings and thoughts. Let your breathing flow freely and observe it attentively.

Direct your attention to the inner space in front of your closed eyes. Let the image of a place of power emerge in this room, a place in nature or at home where you feel really comfortable and safe. Make yourself aware that you can come here at any time; this place is always there for you.

Now, you will enter a deeper level of your being. Somewhere in your place of power you see a passageway. Behind it, there is a staircase with ten steps leading *down* or *inside* your inner being. Step by step, you walk down: ten, nine, eight, seven, six, five, four, three, two, one. Below, you will find a pavilion amid a beautiful garden. Leave the pavilion and walk over the fresh grass. Leaning against a beautiful forged bench, you see a small shovel and a watering can next to it. On the bench seat, there is a preserving jar. You sit down and look at the jar. There is a plant seed inside. Open the jar, and take the seed into your left palm. Bring your sankalpa to mind. If you haven't found it yet, use "I am love" for this exercise. Imagine how a ray of light emerges from the point between your eyebrows and inscribes this information in miniature letters on the seed. The writing begins to shine and sinks into the seed until the whole seed shines, glitters and sparkles with golden light.

Take the small shovel in your right hand and look for a suitable place in the garden where you can plant your sankalpa. Once you have found the spot, look at it for a moment. Say to it: *I bless you with light and love. Thank you for receiving this seed in your fertile soil and helping it to flourish.* Create a small hole in the earth with the shovel very carefully and put the still shining seed in it. Cover it with loose earth. Get the watering can and pour some of the crystalline, glittering, living water in it over the planting place. Look at your work for a moment and then say goodbye.

Slowly walk back through the garden towards the pavilion. On the way, turn around once more. You see a small, bright green leaf emerging from the earth at the spot where you planted the seed. The leaf is already unfolding in the soft sunlight. Smile at it, and then turn around again. Walk through the pavilion and return up the steps to your place of power: one, two, three, four, five, six, seven, eight, nine, ten. Stay there for a moment. Now, prepare to end this exercise. Breathe in deeply, move and stretch yourself pleasurably. Repeat your sankalpa again in a conscious state, and intend to recall it now and then during the day.

CLARIFYING QUESTIONS ON CHAPTER 9

Which of the options mentioned in the course do you think are most likely to be used in your practice?

Repeating your sankalpa at the beginning and end / sankalpa as mantra meditation / visualization of your sankalpa / something else (what?)

On a scale of one to ten, please ask yourself how clearly you see your objectives now in front of you compared to before. How big do you think the difference is?

One to two points / three to five points / more than five points / I don't see any difference

10 THE SANKALPA IN EVERYDAY LIFE

In this chapter, we discuss the methods by which we can support the manifestation of sankalpa in our everyday lives. The three most important are repetition, blessing and letting go of our need for control.

In the last meditation, you planted the seed of your sankalpa in the garden of your subconscious.

This chapter is about how you can support the realization of your heart's desire in your everyday life outside the meditation practice. So, how can you offer this seed the best conditions for growth?

Chapter 7 was about how we can best support the effect of a sankalpa by letting go of everything that prevents us from realizing it. That is an essential element, but we can still do more. To recognize the new opportunities that the germination of the sankalpa will bring to our lives, we should remain as aware as possible of our objective, without, of course, clinging to it. We can achieve this by repeating the sankalpa as often as possible during our day. This works best with a mirror and eye contact with your mirror image. You will undoubtedly remember the mirror exercise in Chapter 3.

Another helpful method for the daily support of sankalpa is a *blessing*. There are certainly many people and animals who would love to have what you want to achieve as well. Inwardly, bless as many beings as possible who you meet in your everyday life with everything that *you* desire. Also bless those who have already achieved it with the ability to enjoy it and use it to the highest good of themselves and the world. With this, you connect yourself to the vibration of this state of being, and it will become ever easier for you to manifest the positive outcome you desire.

The third everyday practice I would like to share with you is the following: Support the achievement of your objective with your conscious actions, but free yourself from the idea of being able to control anything. Here is a short story by well-known Indian Jesuit and wisdom teacher Anthony de Mello:

> A Sufi master and his disciple ride their camels into an oasis town. The master asks the student to look after the camels and enters the guesthouse. The next morning, both camels are gone. When the master asks the disciple what has happened, he says, "Master, you taught me to trust in God. So, I thought I didn't have to attach the camels. God will see to it that they don't run away." The master only says, "Trust in God is good, but we should attach our camels anyway. Why bother Him with what we can do ourselves?"

What can we learn from this story? For example, the following: let's do our best and trust that it will suffice. A sankalpa makes it easier for us to reach an objective. However, that does not mean we mustn't consciously and responsibly follow our own path towards the goal.

EXERCISE 9: THE LIBERATED BREATH / LETTING GO

Today's exercise is about letting go. Set your meditation timer to a time appropriate for you and sit down in your meditation posture. Relax your stomach, shoulders, jaw and tongue. Let your gaze become soft, but keep your eyes half open. Repeat your sankalpa several times, very attentively and in the present.

Now, begin to observe your breathing. Be careful not to influence it. Sometimes, you will find that you are deliberately changing your breathing in some way. Release the impulse as soon as you notice it.

When the time has elapsed, release yourself from the exercise. Repeat your sankalpa several times very attentively and stay present in the moment. Finally, place your hands loosely together in front of your sternum and touch it with your thumbs. Thank yourself for this exercise.

CLARIFYING QUESTIONS ON CHAPTER 10

How often have you repeated the proposed phrases or your sankalpa in recent weeks?

only during the meditation, when it was guided / during and after the meditation, in a conscious state / on most days and in between during everyday life / very often

How important is it to you that your sankalpa is fulfilled?

That would be great; my life will change and improve a lot. / It has to manifest. Otherwise, I can't be happy. / Actually, I don't really believe in it, but let's see.… / I haven't yet found an objective that is really important to me.

11 TURNING WISHES INTO PREFERENCES

In this chapter, we will conclude our journey with a very short excursion into yoga philosophy and a powerful mantra meditation. You will also receive a few tips on how you can, if you wish, continue to work with the list of objectives introduced in this book to make your life even more conscious, self-determined and authentic.

In the last nine chapters, you have been given the tools to understand your desires better and to support their manifestation with the help of consciously formulated sankalpas and objectives. While building the basics for this work, we have realized that the most challenging thing about wishing is often to realize what we actually want. For this purpose, we have used the tool of the list of objectives, where you have listed a multitude of your objectives, regardless of importance or size.

Even if you have found your sankalpa by now (or at least have already come closer to it), you may find on this list even more points that you would like to see realized in your life, but do not yet really know how. If so, it may be beneficial to continue working with the list.

If you want to do that, it's straightforward: get used to writing down the first ten objectives that come to mind every day after your meditation. This will give your subconscious an even better indication of the direction you would like to go than if you were just using your sankalpa, and the subconscious—

often called our "inner child"—will help you. Furthermore, working with the list of objectives also helps you to become more aware of the essentials in your life and to reflect them in your actions. The contents of your list will change. Let yourself be surprised by how exactly this will be. In this practice, it is essential not to look at the list from the previous day before filling it in, to write as spontaneously as possible and only to compare the lists with each other from time to time. This helps us not to drift too much into ego- and intellect-driven considerations, as well as to avoid rigidity and to recognize a change in our objectives as soon as it takes place.

To conclude this book, I would like to share the following thoughts with you: Our conceptually thinking mind, our little ego, has no idea what is really going on here. We think we know, and we *must* think that because it's part of the game—called *lila* in yoga, the game of the Divine absolute with itself.

All mystics tell us the same thing in their own

way: All is good, right here, right now. Finding and keeping this trust is not always easy. However, deep in meditation, we sometimes realize that we are a movement, a wave in this universal field that lacks nothing because it is one with the source.

Therefore, yoga nidra master Satyananda Saraswati recommended the following as the highest (and most courageous) sankalpa of all: *I awaken my Kundalini*. Kundalini is the yogic way to call our personal, individual connection to the original source, an awakening of which brings us more and more back into this clarity and connection to universal love and absolute consciousness and helps us to realize that we have always been at home.

EXERCISE 10: THE AFFIRMATION

Today's exercise is a mantra meditation with the word "Yes" as its object. Set your timer. Sit comfortably in your upright meditation posture. Close your eyes. Take in the word *Yes* in your mind; repeat it very carefully and with complete presence for the duration of the meditation.

When the time is up, let go of the mantra. Breathe freely and naturally. Raise your arms above your head and put your palms together gently. Take a deep breath and then lower your hands with an OOMM in front of your heart. Bow for a moment to your true nature. Say to yourself: Namaste. Thank you; thank you; thank you. I love myself, and I love all being.

CLARIFYING QUESTIONS ON CHAPTER 11

When you hear that your true nature is Divine, what is your first reaction?

I know that in my head, of course, but I am far too rarely aware of it. / That would be nice, but I feel guilty about it. What will the church say? / Nonsense, the Divine is out there and not in me. / Yes, I have been allowed to experience that before.

If an angel were to come by and grant you a single wish, what would he be? Would it be...

already included in your sankalpa / already included in your list of objectives / something new (record immediately ;-) / I'm happy, just as it is

12 THE SANKALPA LIST

To conclude this guide and give you even more material to work with when tracking your own objectives and heartfelt desires, this chapter contains a list of 150 positive impulses - "affirmations" - compiled over the twenty years of my involvement with the subject.

The short phrases presented here come from various sources - including spiritual texts and the writings, lectures and seminars of Louise Hay, Neale Donald Walsch, Ulrich Duprée and Horst Krohne - and may be used either directly as a *sankalpa* or at least as a starting point for discovering your own heart-affirmation. The impulses are arranged according to basic life themes and chakras.

a) Basic Trust in Life and Plenitude (Root Chakra)

I'm free.

Life loves me, and I'm safe.

I am firmly anchored in the fullness of life.

I am safe.

I trust myself, and I trust in life.

I now choose goodness, love and abundance.

I love myself.

I am completely lovable.

I am capable of productive action
and I always give my best.

I am in profound connection
with the earth and the sky.

I am firmly anchored in my
connection to Mother Earth.

I walk the path of love, inside and outside.

I am safe in the universe,
and all being supports me.

I live in abundance and in the flow of life.

I remain in abundance,
no matter what I do or where I go.

I am safe and grateful.

I only eat healthy, nourishing and
lovingly made food.

I feel comfortable in my body.

My body is sacred, a sacred temple.

I love my body.

My body is full of life and vitality.

I deserve the best.

I now choose radiant health in my life.

I can always take good care of myself.

I have the power, the strength and the ability
to cope with everything in life.

It is good and safe to take loving care of myself.

I am good to myself and live in abundance.

b) Relationship and Authenticity (Sacral Chakra)

I let go of all obstacles.

Lovingly, I let go of the past,
and walk on joyfully towards new life experiences.

Full of love I let go of the past and of old beliefs.

I am creative.

My life is full of lightness and joy.

I plant seeds of love and health in my subconscious.

I now choose to open myself

ANDREAS ZIÖRJEN

for healthy and fulfilling relationships.

My heart is open for love and
deeply fulfilling relationships of every kind.

It is safe for me to express love.

I am unconditionally lovable.

It is easy for me to accept love,
from myself and others.

I am complete, I have everything I need.

I bless all beings in my life with love.

I am firmly anchored in self-love
and inner freedom.

Wherever I am, there is joy and laughter.

My contacts with others and the world are close,
loving, nourishing and shaped by mutual respect.

I plant new causes of love and peace
in the garden of my life.

I trust my inner voice and I am relaxed.

I am now resting totally in the love and
joy of my humanity.

I let go of what is holding me and I continue with

ease.

I put myself in the first place in my life.
I permit myself to do that.

I release myself from everything that
robs me of energy.

c) Profession and Vocation (Solar Chakra)

I am full of energy and enthusiasm for life.

Courage and self-esteem are
the pillars of my life.

I decide to handle all of my tasks with
love, lightness and joy.

I am safe in the world of work,
I live in abundance.

I am courageous.

I recognize and live my vocation,
the highest dream of my soul.

113

I let my inner light shine.

I am the master of my life.

I lovingly live my uniqueness
for the good of the whole.

I bless my work with love.

I trust in the best solution
for all participants emerging effortlessly.

I only plant positive thoughts
in the garden of my life.

I plant new seeds of love and peace.

I create only good and positive thoughts.

Only good lies before me.

I live in abundance, and in the flow of life.

I listen to my body and I lovingly
pay attention to its needs.

I have the power, the strength and the possibilities,
to digest anything that touches me.

I choose the path of love.

Each and every one of my actions increases the
vibration of love in the world.

d) Healing and Love (Heart Chakra)

I love myself and my world, unconditionally.

I am full of self-love and in complete inner peace.

I am happy, healthy and whole.

I am filled with gratitude.

I am in harmony with all beings.

I am always connected with the flows of
Divine wisdom and life force.

Healing love and life energy fills every cell of my

body.

I open myself to the spiritual flow of healing.

Namaste. I acknowledge the Divine
in me and in all beings.

I heal my heart, I heal myself
and with this I heal my world.

I now allow my heart
to dissolve all negative beliefs.

I am now totally resting in the love
and joy of my humanity.

My love cleanses my body and all my cells

from negative thoughts about diseases.

I plant seeds of love and health
in the garden of my life.

My love also heals painful memories
stored in my body.

Love flows in every cell of my body.

Peace flows through me, all pressure dissolves.

I allow the infinite well of love in my heart,
to heal everything in me and in my world.

e) Authenticity and Expression (Throat Chakra)

I am completely myself.

I live the highest expression of my soul
every single day.

I love and accept myself with all my
feelings, thoughts, words and actions.

I allow myself to be completely me.

I allow myself to be everything I want to be.

I am always connected with the flow of
Divine inspiration.

I am a loving expression of God's capacity to act.

I radiate love.

I radiate love with all my being.

I radiate love in all my thoughts,
feelings, words and actions.

I live in freedom and love, in clarity,
knowledge and joy.

I forgive myself and all others unconditionally.

I now choose the path of love.

I am always attentive, loving and present,
with myself and all beings I meet.

I am in harmony with all that is.

I am in harmony with all that is and express this
in my thoughts, words and actions.

I now decide to respect all beings, people,
animals and plants.

It is easy and simple.

I increase my vibration with all my
thoughts, words and actions.

I rise above all fear and all competition.

Wherever I am there is a place of peace.

It is safe to follow my inner calling.

I lovingly live my uniqueness
for the good of the whole.

Because I love myself, I only surround
myself with loving people.

I speak only Divine and encouraging words.

I am aware of my creative power.

I fulfil my needs with love and mindfulness.

I let go of all criticism, resistance and prejudice.

I allow myself to always be the best I can be.

f) Clarity and Inner Peace (Third Eye)

I'm all present.

I consciously direct my thoughts
towards all that is good and loving.

I accept my own Divinity.

I allow myself to recognize who I really am.

My thinking is focused on love, joy and happiness.

My action is always guided to the highest good
for myself and for all beings.

I forgive myself and all others unconditionally.

I forgive myself all destructive parts within me
and lovingly let them go.

I am the master of my life.

I move away from old convictions
that no longer suit me with ease.

I now direct my consciousness towards
all good things.

I am now aligning my consciousness with God.

I let go of every thought of lack and failure.

I choose love and life.

I am always loving, attentive and present.

g) Spirituality (Crown Chakra)

I live in lightness, connection and joy.

My vibration becomes higher and higher.

I allow myself to be more
than I now believe I am.

All experiences exclusively serve
the growth of my soul.

I am a channel for the sublime,
I am clear and pure.

I am pure consciousness.

I love myself and I love God / the Great Spirit / the
Great Mother / all being / the universe / your
personal name for the Divine.

I am an inseparable part of God.

I am an important part of God.

I am always in exactly the right place
at the right time.

I am always connected with
the Divine flow of all-embracing wisdom.

I am complete now, I have everything I need.

I rest in the truth and love of God.

I am eternal, spiritual identity.

I am a mirror of the Divine light.

I receive and radiate the love of God.

The Divine source of life
loves me unconditionally.

I am the way, truth and life.

I am the nectar of knowledge, the harmony in
everything and like the vault of heaven.

The contents of this practice book are based on the audio meditation course "Sankalpa", created and guided by Andreas Ziörjen.

EXCERPT FROM "THE INNER GURU'S
PRACTICE BOOK"

by Andreas Ziörjen

Chapter 5

BRINGING MORE LOVE INTO THIS WORLD

What is meditation really about? I suppose there is a
lot of confusion about this. And this is no wonder,
since all of us stand at different places, in our lives, in
our experiences, have to deal with different character
traits, are here in this world for to experience and
learn different things.

In the Yoga Sutra - one of the world's most
important texts on meditation, roughly two-thousand
years old - it is said that the way we meditate and how

deep we can go depends on our primary disposition in life – that is, if we are rather active, introspective or passive beings.

I believe we have a bit more leeway in this, since we're always changing, and therefore our character disposition isn't as fixed a thing either. But, even assuming everyone has the potential to reach the "higher" states of meditation, we still don't know what it's all about. There's active meditation, passive meditation, awareness meditation, mantra meditation, visualization meditation, contemplative meditation, yoga of emotions, movement meditation, active and passive breath meditation, and whatever you want. For almost all of them, there's an exercise in this book you may try out. But what is the common denominator? What is it that makes them *meditation* rather than something else, like psychology, relaxation or just fun?

The Yoga Sutra says on this subject that it's all about quieting the mind. I agree, but again, this is just one kind of meditation, and, there are a lot of interpretations possible what that actually means. Does our mind actually go quiet? Or are we going to a place *behind* the mind, where there is stillness while outside it's still working and doing its everyday chores. This is more like it felt to me in the moments I was going really deep. Or is it that we are becoming *one* with the flow of what is, our sensations, thoughts, words and actions so there is just no difference in our experience anymore between *us* – the ego – and the flow of life, the *now*? Probably, this is all true at the same time. Truth has many faces. And it's difficult or maybe even impossible to capture it in conceptual thinking.

For me, now, meditation is about deep-diving into love. We do this by becoming ever clearer, more present and conscious. We do this by liberating ourselves of destructive patterns and limiting beliefs that stop us from being the loving, open, liberated beings that we already are deep down in our hearts. This, for me, is the meaning of meditation, the path I follow as a practitioner and teacher. Use the exercises in this book to attain more self-love, inner freedom and conscious presence, and not only your whole being – yes, including your ego - will profit from it, but also all the world around us.

Meditation No. 12
from "THE INNER GURU'S PRACTICE BOOK"

METTA BHAVANA MEDITATION

Check into your meditation posture. Observe your breathing and allow it to flow. Focus on the space around your heart. Allow this space to expand. Then, imagine a person or animal that awakens the most positive feeling possible within you. Tell them, in your mind: may you be well. May you be happy. May you be free. Breathe, imagine this coming to pass for that being, imagine how it might be. Hold this image and breathe. Then, turn your gaze further inward towards yourself. Tell yourself: May you be well. May you be happy. May you be free. Imagine yourself being, completely well, happy and free. Breathe. Then, do the same with a neutral person, say the waitress at a restaurant you recently visited, then with a person you don't like very much, and lastly with the person that you dislike most at the moment (if there is one). You may extend this exercise to as many persons or animals you like. To finish this exercise, you may visualize the earth and do the same with it and all beings on it, all human, animal, plant and mineral life.

ABOUT THE AUTHOR

Andreas Ziörjen is the author of several books on meditation, yoga philosophy and deep relaxation, including "On How to Become Your Own Guru," an in-depth exploration on the tantric principles of all meditative paths and the value of non-dogmatic spirituality. For more than twenty years he has been intensively engaged in yoga, meditation and new spirituality. In his work as a seminar leader and therapist, he is particularly interested in the transfer of spirituality into everyday life and the development of a new view of success and self-love beyond performance and self-optimization.

His primary practice is yoga nidra, in which sankalpa plays an important role. For many years Andreas has also been involved with Ho'oponopono, the path of forgiveness and inner peace originally from Hawaii, in which the conscious handling of thoughts and intentions ("mana mana") also is of central significance.

Guided meditations to download, more information about

Andreas' workshops and retreats, as well as the possibility to
book appointments in Ho'oponopono, craniosacral therapy,
yoga therapy or aura-energetics may be found on the following
websites:

www.andreasziorjen.com
(international site in English and German)

www.yogatherapie-thun.ch
(local site for meditation and holistic healing in
Thun, Switzerland, German-only)

www.andreasziorjen.photoshelter.com
(more information about Andreas' artwork)

**Explore a new, powerful way to harmonize all
areas of your life**

The *Chakra-Course*, Andreas' most in-depth online
series, offers over six hours of audio content,
including nine advanced, chakra-specific yoga-nidra
exercises helping you to deep-dive into the self-
healing capacities of your body and mind.

Each practice is designed to be practiced daily for at
least a week before moving on to the next one. This
allows you to truly feel its effects and integrate its full
potential.

Try it risk-free for 90 days. The course will be
available from spring 2019 for download in the web
shop on www.andreasziorjen.com

How can we manifest our dreams?
**And how can we really know what our dreams
are?**

In the *Sankalpa-Course* you will learn more about this
in ten guided fifteen-minute sessions, each containing
a combination of theory and practical application in a
short meditation exercise.

Join Andreas in exploring how to recognize and
connect to your deepest needs and desires, and how
to best ask your subconscious to assist in their
manifestation into reality.

The course will be available from spring 2019 on

www.andreasziorjen.com

BOOKS BY ANDREAS ZIÖRJEN

On How to Become Your Own Guru - Find Your Way Towards a
More Effective Meditation, Yoga or Qigong Practice

The Inner Guru's Practice Book – 37 Meditations for Yoga
Teachers and Practitioners

Sankalpa - How to Understand and Manifest your Innermost
Desires

**Audio-Meditations and Courses, for download on
www.chakra-atelier.ch**

Yoga-Nidra

Yoga-Nidra with Ho'oponopono for Self-Forgiveness

Yoga-Nidra for Inner Harmony

Yoga-Nidra for Sleep

Meditations

Radiating Love Meditation

Freedom of Breath Meditation

Positive Thought Meditation

Courses

The Sankalpa Course

The Chakra Course (with Yoga-Nidra)

Andreas is teaching on *Insight Timer* too, one of the world's
leading free meditation apps. Check it out.

NAMASTE.

OM SHANTI, SHANTI, SHANTI.

MAY LOVE AND PEACE PREVAIL ON EARTH.

E HO'OMALUHIA ME KA HONUA.

Made in the
USA
Monee, IL